Editor
David Cook

Editorial Project Manager
Ina Massler Levin, M.A.

Editor in Chief
Sharon Coan, M.S. Ed.

Illustrator
Howard Chaney

Cover Artist
Sue Fullam

Art Coordinator
Denice Adorno

Creative Director
Elayne Roberts

Imaging
Ralph Olmedo, Jr.

Product Manager
Phil Garcia

Publishers
Rachelle Cracchiolo, M.S. Ed.
Mary Dupuy Smith, M.S. Ed.

How to Write a Sentence

Grades 1–3

Author

Kathleen Christopher Null

Teacher Created Materials, Inc.
6421 Industry Way
Westminster, CA 92683
www.teachercreated.com

Reprinted, 2000 b
Made in U.S.A.
ISBN-1-57690-498-9

Table of Contents

Introduction

This book will enable you to teach your students the basics of sentence writing in an enjoyable and memorable fashion. The first section, Presenting the Sentence! (pages 6–10), provides a foundation for the activities in the sections which follow. Each page in this section provides basic information about sentences which you may pass on to your students in whatever manner best suits their abilities and needs. For those students who are already sentence savvy, you may wish to have them read the pages and do the activities independently. In such a case, you may find it advantageous to reproduce selected answers from the Answer Key (pages 46–48) and make them available to students for self-checking. Expand on the activities and instruction if your students are having difficulty with a particular concept, or simply choose only those activities that are needed to enrich learning. What Is a Sentence? (pages 6 and 7) and Can You Find the Sentences? (page 8) familiarize students with the basic components required in each sentence and allow them to strengthen that knowledge by distinguishing sentences from nonsentences. Can You Fix These Sentences? (page 9) gives the students the opportunity to be sentence mechanics as they use the tools that are now familiar to them to practice their editing skills. Sentence Starters (page 10) is a creative activity that allows students to show how much they have learned about writing basic sentences. In the first part of the activity, they simply finish sentences that have already been started for them. In the second part of the activity, they work at filling in the missing information.

The Bigger and Better Sentences section (pages 11–15) begins with a two-page introduction to run-on sentences, Stop That Run-On Sentence! (pages 11–12). The activities for run-on sentences are followed by two exercises on sentence fragments. Broken Sentences (pages 13 and 14) begins with some lighthearted instruction on fragments and then moves on to two activities for students to practice identifying and adding the missing information to fragmented sentences. To sum it all up, Which Is Which? (page 15) is an activity to help students identify both sentence fragments and run-on sentences.

The Polishing Your Sentences section (pages 16–21) begins with the basics of capitalization, Capital Letters (pages 16 and 17). You may wish to make an enlarged copy on brightly-colored paper to hang on the wall for easy reference. Also included is a fun coloring activity to reinforce the use of the capital letter I. How Does It End? (page 18) is an activity to reinforce what has been learned about punctuation at the ends of sentences. To expand upon this activity, you may wish to have students punctuate sentences that are written on the board or on a long piece of butcher paper.

Introduction *(cont.)*

Take a Breath! (pages 19 and 20) begins with a page that covers some basic punctuation rules. You may wish to enlarge the rules and post them in the classroom. In the activity, students have the opportunity to practice all the punctuation they have learned so far. You may wish to make punctuation fun by assigning various sounds to the punctuation marks (e.g., a popping sound for periods, a "zing" for commas, etc.). Then as the whole class reads aloud, students can call out the punctuation sounds. For the final polish, Make Your Sentences Come Alive! (page 21) is a very basic introduction to modifiers and descriptive adverbs and adjectives to increase the students' sentence-writing abilities.

What's It About? (pages 22–25) is a section devoted to sentence subjects. The first activity, This Sentence Is About . . . (page 22), introduces your students to the concept that all sentences are about someone or something. To expand the activity, make sentence strips for the whole class. Omit the subjects from sentences and allow the students to supply them. Subject Search (page 23) reinforces what has been learned about subjects as students are introduced to a formula for determining the subject of any sentence. Can You Find the Subject? (page 24) provides another approach as students search for subjects in the sentences presented on the page. An amusing activity which will also reinforce learning is Can You Put the Subject in a Sentence? (page 25). Students choose subjects to add to sentences and write some sentences of their own as well.

What Happens? (pages 26–29) is a section devoted to the predicate. Your students will recognize predicates and realize their importance when they do the first activity, We Need a Predicate! (page 26). Your Turn to Add the Predicate (page 27) reinforces what has been learned about predicates as students create silly sentences. Now Put Them Together (pages 28 and 29) is a matching game that can be played individually or in groups.

It Couldn't Happen Without a Verb (pages 30–33) is a section dedicated to the verb and its importance to a sentence. The first activity, Two Kinds of Verbs (page 30), begins with an introduction to active and passive verbs and then allows students the opportunity to recognize verbs in sentences. Action! (page 31) is an activity in which students read a short paragraph and circle all the action verbs they can find. Verb Hunt (page 32) is an activity that allows students to search for verbs among other kinds of words. A paragraph missing some verbs appears on page 33, Calling All Verbs! Students will read the paragraph and choose verbs from the word bank to complete the story.

Introduction *(cont.)*

Describe It! (pages 34–38) is a section devoted to the adjective. Adjectives Revisited (page 34) is an activity that reinforces what students learned in an earlier section, and introduces them to further concepts in this section. Find the Adjectives (page 35) is an activity that will test students' recognition of adjectives. Students locate the adjectives among the nouns and verbs and circle them. To extend the activity, you may want to present students with the challenge of creating sentences with the words found on this page. Students can add their own adjectives to the story on page 36, Your Turn to Create Adjectives. If they need inspiration, or if they are just learning, they may rely on the word bank at the bottom of the page. Matching Adjectives (pages 37 and 38) is a matching game that matches adjectives with words they might modify.

In the final section of the book, Sentence Fun! (pages 39–44), the activities are designed for students to have fun while reinforcing what they've learned. The first activity, One Sentence at a Time (page 39), starts with the sentence, "It was a dark and stormy night." Each student writes the sentence that comes next and then finds classmates or family members (if assigned as homework) to add the sentences that follow. When the activity has been completed, you can have the class read aloud and compare the stories. Sentence Maze (page 40) is a change of pace that allows students to have fun while calling upon their basic knowledge of sentence structure in order to solve the puzzle. Silly Sentences (pages 41–43) is another fun activity. Follow the directions for an inspiring game, and then students can write stories based on their favorite silly sentences. Matching games could also be played with these cards if you wish. All About Me! (page 44) is a sentence-writing activity that gives students the opportunity to write about their favorite subjects—themselves! While writing about themselves, they may not notice that they are incorporating what they have learned in this book to write sentences. You will find an award on page 45, which you can reproduce and present to students, congratulating them for their sentence-writing efforts.

What Is a Sentence?

A sentence begins with a capital letter.

Examples:

My cat ate my homework.

A big dragon sat on my head.

You wouldn't write sentences like these:

my cat ate my homework.

a big dragon sat on my head.

Sentences end with punctuation: a period (.), a question mark (?), or an exclamation point (!). A period should be used to end most sentences. Use a question mark when the sentence asks a question, and use the exclamation point when the sentence is expressing something very angry, very exciting, very important, or very urgent.

Here are some examples of sentences that end with periods:

My dog has fleas.

I don't eat broccoli.

Here are some examples of sentences that end with question marks:

Did you know that my dog has fleas?

Why did you put broccoli in this?

Here are some examples of sentences that end with exclamation points:

My dog has fleas again!

I told you, I don't ever eat broccoli!

There is one more thing you need to know about sentences: A sentence is always a complete thought. The following are not complete thoughts, so they are not sentences:

My cat

If I am

Do you want

What Is a Sentence? *(cont.)*

These are complete thoughts, and they have capital letters at the beginnings and punctuation marks at the ends, so they are sentences:

My cat is sleeping on top of the refrigerator.

Do you want to go look at the dragon with me?

Now write a sentence of your own. Make sure it starts with a capital letter and ends with a period, a question mark, or an exclamation point. Is it a complete thought? If not, what can you add to make it a complete thought?

You have learned that every sentence must have a capital letter at the beginning and a period, question mark, or exclamation point at the end. Every sentence must also be a complete thought.

Circle the sentences below.

1. all through the town
2. I hate broccoli!
3. Are you afraid of dragons?
4. I will hop on one foot for three days!
5. Are you under the bed?
6. I don't like
7. I saw Tiffany swimming by.
8. Can I cut your hair?
9. This cheese tastes
10. Let's go jump on the bed!

Now write three sentences of your own. End one with a period, one with a question mark, and one with an exclamation point. Make sure that your sentences are complete thoughts.

1. ____

2. ____

3. ____

Can You Find the Sentences?

A sentence is a group of words that tells us something or asks us a question. It is always a complete thought. Each sentence is about someone or something. Each sentence also tells us something about someone or something.

Example: John cooks dinner.

This is what the sentence tells us:

Who it is about: *John*

What John does: *cooks dinner*

There are only five complete sentences below. Can you find them? Remember, sentences begin with capital letters, end with punctuation (a period, question mark, or exclamation point), and contain a complete thought that tells us about something or someone. Write the five sentences on the lines below.

Chris is making enchiladas!	You don't know what
telling me a story.	My dog went ice skating.
Stop that runaway bicycle!	When I stop.
How about that one who	when will you know?
Do you like cotton candy	Kip is washing the dishes.
Give Jason	A big, yellow house.
I like Mike!	the wind

1. ______________________________

2. ______________________________

3. ______________________________

4. ______________________________

5. ______________________________

Can You Fix These Sentences?

Help! The sentences below are broken! Can you fix them? Below each broken sentence, write the new, complete sentence. Remember to use a period, a question mark, or an exclamation point to end each one. The first one has been done for you.

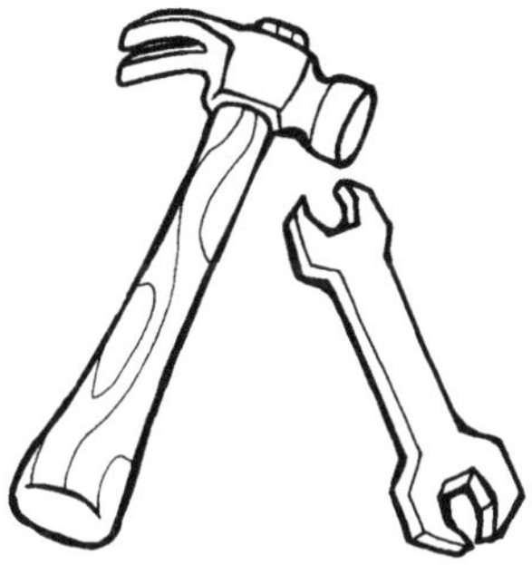

1. can I get a kitten

   Can I get a kitten? ______________________

2. watch out, kevin

   ____

3. i won a prize

   ____

4. will you be my best friend

   ____

5. in the morning, I will

   ____

6. what's for lunch

   ____

7. we were taking a bath

   ____

8. a giant dragonfly landed on my head

   ____

Sentence Starters

Finish these sentences any way you like.

1. Maggie wants to ____

2. Do you ____

3. I wish I had____

4. Have you ever ____

5. Watch out for the ____

Finish these sentences by filling in the blanks.

1. ______________________________________is a big, hairy monster!

2. Did you say that your ___________________________________fell off?

3. _____________ jumped into the spaghetti and then _______________!

4. _____________________ is trying to find ____________________.

5. A ____________________ is knocking on the ___________________.

Stop That Run-On Sentence!

You've learned that each sentence is a complete thought. Some sentences may have too many thoughts and may not give you a chance to catch your breath. What do you think of this sentence?

I was walking to school school is fun I really like it.

It's easy to see that there are too many thoughts there for one sentence. This is called a "run-on sentence." It ought to read like this:

I was walking to school. School is fun. I really like it.

Here are some more run-on sentences. Put a line between the complete thoughts in each sentence. It helps to say them out loud and listen for the places where you pause to take a breath. The first two have been done for you.

1. My dog jumped over the fence/she ran away with a poodle.
2. When I got home from school, my little brother was wearing my hat/ I do not like it when he does that/ he chews and drools on my hat/ he is teething.
3. My teacher is nice she smiles all day long.
4. I got some new goggles do you want to go swimming?
5. My brother is sick he has to take some nasty smelling medicine.
6. I have a hamster her name is Stella.
7. Pizza is my favorite food my sister works at Pizzaland.
8. Can I go over to Lan's house we're going to play space rockets it's a really fun game you would like it do you want to come and watch us?
9. I got a new bicycle it is blue and white it goes really fast I like it a lot.
10. There is a snake in my classroom at school I like toads and frogs better my friend Nathan prefers mice.

Stop That Run-On Sentence! *(cont.)*

You have learned that each sentence is a complete thought and that a sentence that runs on to the next thought is called a run-on sentence. Here is an example.

Run-on: Cake is my favorite dessert chocolate is my favorite flavor.
Correct: Cake is my favorite dessert. Chocolate is my favorite flavor.

Each of the following sentences is a run-on sentence. You can fix them by making them into two sentences instead of one. The first two have been done for you.

1. I want lots of stories tonight can you start with Cinderella?

   I want lots of stories tonight. Can you start with Cinderella?
2. Come over to my house we can have some ice cream.

   Come over to my house. We can have some ice cream.
3. I got a new scooter wait until you see it!

   ____
4. I don't want any soup it's too hot.

   ____
5. My baby brother ate my homework he was very hungry.

   ____
6. Carrie saw a monster in the park he was afraid of her.

   ____
7. My mom got new shoes I tried them on.

   ____
8. My cat scratched me do you have a cat?

   ____
9. Hector planted some flower seeds weeds grew instead of flowers.

   ____
10. Can you come to my birthday party we'll have lots of fun.

    ____

Broken Sentences

You have learned that a sentence must be a complete thought. If it's not, it isn't a sentence. It also doesn't make much sense.

Example:

How do you

My little brother

There is something missing in each of these examples. These are called sentence fragments. They are just some pieces of sentences. When the missing pieces are added, they will be complete sentences. What is missing in the fragments above? Here are some ideas:

How do you [*do something*]?

My little brother [*did something, said something, or is something*].

When you think of these ideas, you can make them into complete sentences:

How do you *expect me to sleep with you snoring so loudly?*

My little brother *is an alien from the planet Zorkin.*

Fill in the blanks below to make these fragments into complete sentences.

1. My best friend ____.
2. I saw ____.
3. ____ ate a bug this morning.
4. A big, scary ____.
5. ____ fell into the trash can.
6. I ran out of the ____.
7. We don't want to ____.
8. Tell me about ____.

Broken Sentences *(cont.)*

You've learned a lot about sentences so far. Are you ready for a challenge?

There are five groups of words on this page. They all need some help. Some are fragments and some are sentences. They all need capitals at the beginning and punctuation at the ends (a period, a question mark, or an exclamation point). Your job is to write the complete sentences with the correct capital letters and punctuation. If the sentence is a fragment, you must use your imagination to add the missing information.

1. tasha is in her bedroom

   ____

   ____

2. two stuffed animals

   ____

   ____

3. do you see the toys under the bed

   ____

   ____

4. my favorite game

   ____

   ____

5. look out for

   ____

   ____

Which Is Which?

Can you tell the difference between a run-on sentence and a sentence fragment? Just to remind you, here's a hint: A run-on sentence is too much. A sentence fragment is not enough.

For the word groups below, put an F for a fragment or an R for a run-on on the line before the sentence. In the space below each group, write the sentences as they should be written. Complete the sentence fragments, provide punctuation, and break up the run-ons.

______1. Come on, let's

____

____

______2. My book is

____

____

______3. I stubbed my big toe it hurt a lot.

____

____

______4. A yellow airplane

____

____

______5. The story was funny I couldn't check it out of the library I forgot my library card.

____

____

Capital Letters

A B C D E F G H I J K L M N O P Q R S T U V W X Y Z

a b c d e f g h i j k l m n o p q r s t u v w x y z

If you look up, you may see these letters in your classroom. You know these letters very well and can probably still remember how to sing the alphabet song. Without these letters, you would not be able to read your favorite book or write a note to your best friend. Now it's time to learn when to use the uppercase, or capital, letters, and when to use the lowercase letters. You use the uppercase letters to capitalize. To capitalize, you begin a word with a capital, or uppercase, letter. Here is a list of things you should always capitalize:

- **The word "I"**
  When I get home I will eat lunch.
- **The first word in a sentence**
  Tell me a story!
- **The names of people and places (proper nouns)**
  Jennifer Mexico
- **Words derived from proper nouns (proper adjectives)**
  German African
- **Titles with people's names (titles of position, rank, etc.)**
  Doctor Tracy Mrs. Hernandez
- **Titles when used in place of a person's name**
  Did Coach cancel practice?
- **Days of the week and months**
  Monday July
- **The first word in a letter to a friend or relative**
  Dear Anna Dear Friends
- **The first letter of each word in a business letter greeting**
  To Whom It May Concern:
  Dear Students:
- **The main words in titles of books, movies, newspapers, television shows, plays, operas, musicals, or magazines**
  A Wrinkle in Time Newsweek
- **School subjects if they are languages or actual class titles listed in a catalog**
  English Spanish
  Modern American Art
- **Geographic locations when they name specific areas**
  She comes from the North.
- **Holidays**
  Fourth of July Halloween

Capital Letters *(cont.)*

Insert the missing words in each rainbow sentence and lightly color each band with the color used in the sentence. Remember: Always capitalize the word I.

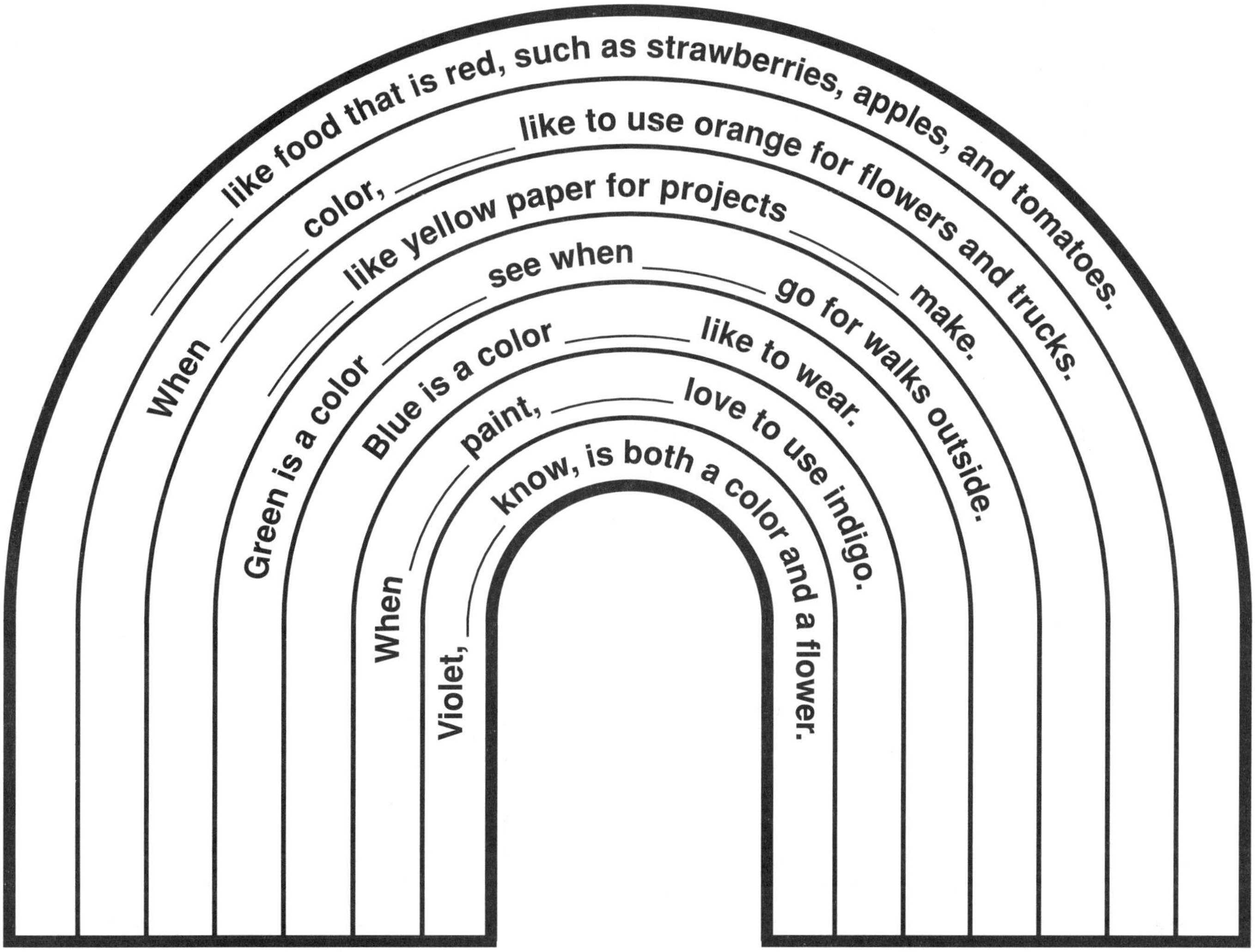

How Does It End?

As you have been learning, each sentence you write must end with a punctuation mark. A sentence may end with a period (.), a question mark (?), or an exclamation point (!).

- A period comes at the end of a sentence that just tells something.

  Examples:

  I have a big dog. I live in a blue house.

- A question mark comes at the end of a sentence that asks a question.

  Examples:

  What is your name? Is your hair green?

- An exclamation point comes at the end of a sentence that contains a strong feeling.

  Examples:

  Get down from there! I can't wait!

The following sentences need end marks. Think about what kind of punctuation each sentence needs: a period, a question mark, or an exclamation point. When you think you know, put the appropriate mark in the box at the end of each sentence.

1. My dog has spots
2. I hate lima beans
3. Do you have a skateboard
4. I am writing a book
5. Who painted my toenails orange
6. My cat can sing
7. I'm sleepy
8. Have you ever visited the planet Teflor
9. Turn that radio down
10. I would like some more, please

Take a Breath!

Punctuation is important when you write a sentence. Without punctuation, the reader doesn't know whether to keep reading, pause for breath, or stop. You are already familiar with periods, question marks, and exclamation points. Now you will learn about commas, apostrophes, colons, and quotation marks.

You should use a comma (,):

- to indicate a pause between adjectives, clauses, phrases, or combined sentences. Examples:

  Even after our vacation, I still wanted to rest.

  My brother has a large, yellow, shaggy dog.
- to separate a city and a state. Example: Denver, Colorado
- to separate the day and year in a date. Example: November 13, 1998
- to separate three or more words or phrases in a list or series.

  Example: I like the colors blue, green, and red.
- after the name of a person to whom you are speaking.

  Example: Jeremy, I see you.
- to set off phrases or words that interrupt the main thought in a sentence.

  Example: I, of course, couldn't sit still.
- to separate who is talking from what is being said.

  Examples: She asked, "What are you doing?" "I'm not going to tell you," I said.

You should use an apostrophe ('):

- to stand for the missing letters in contractions.

  Example: it's, you've, I'm
- to indicate possession. Examples: David's umbrella, a plumber's tools

You should use a colon (:):

- to introduce a list.

  Example: Bring the following: pencils, paper, glue, and a ruler.
- to introduce a long quotation.

  Example: Mother said: Please remember to brush your teeth before school this morning. You've forgotten for three days in a row, and if you don't start brushing, your teeth are all going to fall out.

Take a Breath! *(cont.)*

Here are some sentences that are not punctuated:

> Will you be coming to my birthday party My dad said Calvin Clown will be visiting your birthday party Dont tell anybody but its really my daddy dressed up as a clown I saw him trying on the clown costume and I saw his funny red nose under the bed Its going to be so much fun You will be able to come wont you

Did you find a place to take a breath? Here are the same words with punctuation. You might want to try reading out loud and making a special sound for each punctuation mark.

> Will you be coming to my birthday party? My dad said, "Calvin Clown will be visiting your birthday party!" Don't tell anybody, but it's really my daddy dressed up as a clown. I saw him trying on the clown costume, and I saw his funny red nose under the bed. It's going to be so much fun! You will be able to come, won't you?

Now it's your turn to try punctuating sentences. Use periods, question marks, exclamation points, commas, apostrophes, colons, and quotation marks. If you need help, look at the punctuation rules as a reminder.

1. I said I don t want to go to the dentist
2. I found these things in my backpack rubber bands a popsicle stick a rubber ducky my dog s leash and a doggie biscuit
3. Do you know how to spell shouldn t
4. My mom said Clean up your room right now or you won t be going out
5. Ouch that hurt
6. Tanya can I talk to you
7. When my sister saw the spider she yelled Yikes
8. The new boy Jacob comes from Phoenix Arizona
9. I have four pets a dog a cat a goldfish and an iguana
10. Help she s standing on my hair

Make Your Sentences Come Alive!

You have learned how to write a simple, complete sentence. Now it's time to learn how to make your sentences come alive. Adjectives and adverbs are the spices you can use to make your sentences more interesting. Here are some sentences without adjectives or adverbs:

The lady ran from the bee. Timothy hid from the dog.

Here are the same sentences spiced up with adjectives and adverbs:

The short lady ran quickly from the buzzing bee. Timothy hid quietly from the snarling dog.

An adjective is a word that is used to describe a person, place, or thing. What kind of lady ran from the bee? A short lady. What kind of bee? A buzzing bee! An adverb is a word used to describe a verb (an action word). How did the lady run from the bee? She ran quickly! How did Timothy hide? He hid quietly!

In the sentences below there are spaces for you to make up your own describing words. If you get stuck, you can use the adjectives and adverbs listed below.

Adjectives: big, green, snarling, sleepy, slippery, old, soft, fuzzy, sticky, crunchy, striped, grouchy, hissing, crazy, slimy, confused, messy, loud

Adverbs: quickly, slowly, sadly, happily, gleefully, sleepily, angrily, wickedly, lovingly, softly, silently, loudly, frightfully, nicely, peacefully, beautifully

1. My ______________ (adjective) hamster ate a(n) ______________ (adjective) grape ______________ (adverb).

2. Get up ______________ (adverb) and make a(n) ______________ (adjective) birthday card.

3. The ______________ (adjective) teacher ran ______________ (adverb) from the room when the ______________ (adjective) snake crawled under her desk!

4. My ______________ (adjective), ______________ (adjective) brother told me to go ______________ (adverb) to the store to get his ______________ (adjective) candy bar.

This Sentence Is About . . .

You have learned that all sentences are complete. To be complete, a sentence must be about someone or something. The someone or something that a sentence is about is called the subject. The subject is the main part of the sentence. Without a subject, there is no sentence. Here are some groups of words that do not have subjects. Can these really be sentences? No!

my favorite talks too much

When a subject is added to the sentence, it makes sense:

My favorite color is blue. Friday is my favorite day. (Note that the subject does not always have to come first in a sentence.)

My neighbor talks too much. I told my sister she talks too much.

Add subjects to these sentences. The first two have been done for you.

1. I like donuts.
   Who likes donuts? I like donuts.
2. My favorite subject is math.
   What is my favorite subject? Math is my favorite subject.
3. ______________________________ swims very well.
   Who swims very well? ______________________________
4. My favorite color is ______________________________.
   What is my favorite color? ______________________________
5. ______________________________ really enjoys going to the playground.
   Who really enjoys going to the playground? ______________________________
6. On Saturdays, my ______________________________ takes me to the movies.
   Who takes me to the movies on Saturdays? ______________________________
7. ______________________________ is my best friend.
   Who is my best friend? ______________________________
8. The ______________________________ fell off the table. ______________
   What fell off the table? ______________________________

Subject Search

The subject is who or what the sentence is about. When an artist creates a painting of a vase full of colorful flowers set upon a white cloth in front of a blue background, the subject of the painting is the vase of colorful flowers. The rest of the painting just gives more information about the vase of flowers. Here is how it works with sentences.

Example:

Swimming is fun.

What is fun? *Swimming* is fun.

The subject of this sentence is swimming.

In the sentences below, ask yourself who or what the sentence is about. Underline the subject of the sentence and write the subject of the sentence on the line. If you need help, try answering the question about each sentence first. The first one has been done for you.

1. Puppies love to run.
   What loves to run? *Puppies*
2. My ice cream is melting!
   What is melting? ______________
3. Jason is at school.
   Who is at school? ______________
4. Your dad is really tall!
   Who is really tall? ______________
5. Christy wants to swim.
   Who wants to swim? ______________
6. Jacob's nose is green!
   What is green? ______________
7. The baby is smeared with peanut butter!
   Who is smeared with peanut butter? ______________
8. Mark's hair is falling off!
   What is falling off? ______________
9. Kip really does not like tomatoes!
   Who doesn't like tomatoes?
   ____
10. The telephone is ringing!
    What is ringing? ______________

Can You Find the Subject?

A big storm has blown the subjects away from their sentences! Can you find them and bring them back? Put the subjects back in the sentences where they belong.

1. My ______________ brings me home.		Summer
2. The ______________ tastes very good.		Blue
3. My ________________ can run very fast.		cat
4. The ______________ likes to sleep on my bed.		pie
5. The ___________________ is too loud!		sister
6. Do _______________________ like this book?		you
7. _______________________ is my favorite color		television
8. _______________________ is my favorite time of year.		mother

Can You Put the Subject in a Sentence?

You have learned about subjects and how important they are in your sentences. Now it's time to create your own subjects. These sentences are missing their subjects. Can you add the missing subjects? Be creative.

1. ______________________________ sat on the bowl of soup.
2. ______________________________ picked up a snake, and it bit him!
3. ______________________ came down from the sky, and we got all wet!
4. My brand new ________________________ is broken already.
5. _________________________________ slipped on a patch of ice.
6. Your _______________________________ is falling off!
7. _______________________________ is running away!
8. ____________________________________is what I am eating.

Now use these subjects to write sentences. Don't forget punctuation!

1. lizard ____
2. peanut butter ____
3. old shoes ____
4. crayons____
5. snowballs ____
6. toenails____
7. skateboard ____
8. telephone booth ____

Now you are ready to write your own sentences. On the back of this page, write three sentences about yourself or your family. Underline the subject of each of your sentences.

We Need a Predicate!

You've learned that all sentences have subjects. They also need predicates. The predicate is the part of a sentence that tells us something about the subject. The predicate tells us what the subject does, has, or is.

Examples:

Lucy has a cold.

Lucy is the subject. What does Lucy have? Lucy has a cold.

The predicate is *has a cold.*

Erik jumps into the lake.

Erik is the subject. What does Erik do? Erik jumps into the lake.

The predicate is *jumps into the lake.*

Kyle is a good student.

Kyle is the subject. What is Kyle? Kyle is a good student.

The predicate is *is a good student.*

In the sentences below, underline the subjects. After you have underlined the subjects, ask yourself what the subject does, has, or is. Circle the predicates. The first two have been done for you.

1. Lisette is a good baseball player.
2. We went to the park.
3. My dog likes to chew on my shoes.
4. Jamie has a tree house.
5. My grandma made me a birthday cake.
6. Tasha swims really fast.
7. I don't like Brussels sprouts.
8. My brother is too noisy.
9. I like to eat fish.
10. Tony's feet are really big!

Your Turn to Add the Predicate

Here are some sentences that are missing predicates. Choose a predicate from the box to complete each sentence. The first one has been done for you.

The following predicates may be used more than once.

has a cute little hat.	ran on the playground.	was under the house.
is very gross.	snores.	is as big as Australia.
is drooling.	fell on my toe.	is a spy.
has an attitude.	is growling.	floats away.
is crying.	is singing in an opera.	is purple with polka dots.
climbs on the furniture.	is really an alien.	drove over the hills.
is lost in space.	is covered in stripes.	is growing.

1. My kitten is singing in an opera.
2. Mrs. Crabapple ______________________________.
3. A giant elephant ______________________________.
4. My little brother ______________________________.
5. The grizzly bear ______________________________.
6. A jet plane ______________________________.
7. The science book ______________________________.
8. Your nose ______________________________.
9. My dad ______________________________.
10. My school ______________________________.

Now Put Them Together

Students may play this matching game by themselves or with a partner.

Preparation: Reproduce this page and the next, one copy for each student or pair of students. Cut out the subject and predicate strips. Glue them onto 3" x 5" (8 cm x 13 cm) index cards. Allow the glue to dry. Cut out the directions, and place a copy with each set of game cards.

Directions: Shuffle the cards and place them facedown in random order. Turn a card over and look at it. Turn another card over. If the two cards go together to make a complete sentence, keep them. If they do not make a complete sentence, turn both of them back over. If you are playing by yourself, try again. You win when you have made as many matched pairs as possible. If you are playing with someone else, take turns with your partner. The winner is the player holding the greatest number of matched pairs.

Challenge: At the end of the game, tell whether each card you have in your hand is a subject or a predicate.

Subject Cards

Jamie	the octopus	my ears
Ms. Newton	my pizza	your sister
your crayon	Mr. Martinez	a washing machine
your hair	Sammy the Snake	your big toe
my lollipop	my homework	Liza
the window	my thumb	the fire engine
my bed	my lunch	the class
a wading pool	the ice cream cone	the bathtub
the laughing bunny	your nose	my hamster
a spaceship	that yucky lima bean	Governor Fish

Now Put Them Together *(cont.)*

Predicate Cards

is asleep	should be put away
needs to be washed	itches
is upside down	hangs from my ceiling
is my favorite	will sing
is standing right next to you	should be eaten
is not a good idea	likes me
runs down the street	has a bad cold
is delicious	is in my pocket
is stuck to the wall	needs to be fed
went to Mars	falls apart
had so much fun	twirls in circles
has a friend	is ticklish
is yellow	can talk
ran in your yard	dances on the driveway
is on my head	is in my ear

Two Kinds of Verbs

Verbs are very important to sentences. Did you notice that a predicate always has a verb? Verbs tell what the subject does, or they tell what a subject has or is.

There are two kinds of verbs. There are action verbs and nonaction verbs. It's very easy to tell an action verb because it is all about action. Action verbs are words like run, jump, cry, kick, walk, laugh, etc.

Here is an example of an action verb:

Kip runs home.

What does Kip do? runs

The action verb is *runs.*

A nonaction verb links the subject with another word or phrase by telling what the subject has or is.

Here is an example of a nonaction verb:

Jason has lots of marbles.

The nonaction verb is *has.*

In the sentences below, circle all of the verbs that you find. There are both action and nonaction verbs in the sentences. The first one has been done for you.

1. My cat has fleas.
2. I ran to your house!
3. Kip has a nice dog.
4. Yoshi kicks the ball.
5. My name is Amy.
6. Dr. Williams is nice.
7. My dog jumped over the fence!
8. My sister screamed on the roller coaster.
9. Your face is dirty.
10. I fell off the bed!

Action!

An action verb tells what the subject does.

Examples: run, swing, jump, laugh, see, hit, leap

What are some of your favorite action verbs? Write them here: ______________

____

In the following paragraph there are 21 action verbs. Can you find at least 9 of them? All of the verbs in the paragraph are underlined. Your job is to find the action verbs and circle them. Remember, nonaction verbs are also underlined, so don't be fooled. When you find an action verb, write it in the box at the bottom of the page.

My big sister and I were playing hide and seek. Pablo, our next-door neighbor, ran over to our house. He played with us, too. Pablo is really big. My sister is really smart. I have a good hiding place. My sister counted to 100. She yelled the numbers. Pablo tried very hard. Pablo hid behind the truck. I hid under the house. My sister found Pablo. They looked for me. They looked everywhere. I was tired of waiting. I meowed like a kitten. My sister looked under the house. I growled at her. She screamed! We all laughed. After that we all ate ice cream. "We should play again!" I said. We ran back into the front yard!

Action Verbs

______________	______________	______________
______________	______________	______________
______________	______________	______________

Verb Hunt

There are 10 verbs in the box. Can you find them all? Circle the verbs you find and add one to each of the sentences below. You can write them wherever they seem to fit. Notice that some words can be used as verbs or nouns.

dog	fall	kick
run	cat	pencil
walk	dinner	candy
purple	cute	sad
sleep	tickle	hug
big	tree	picture
football	black	bug
nose	sneeze	car
jump	shoe	dance
book	tiny	rug

1. I will ______________________________ on your head, now!
2. Hey, don't ______________________________ my eye!
3. We should ______________________________ right into the soup!
4. May I ______________________________ on your back?
5. Will you ______________________________ on the roof?
6. I always ______________________________when the telephone rings!
7. Don't ______________________________ the ball toward the windows.
8. Why don't you ______________________________ everyone?
9. I will ______________________________ all day long!
10. You should ______________________________ some more!

Calling All Verbs!

The story below is missing some of its verbs! It's not easy to tell a story without verbs. Your job is to add verbs to make it a story. Some of the verbs are there, and they are underlined. You may use the word bank below for ideas to fill in the missing words. (Words from the word bank can be used more than once.)

Word Bank

watched	put	poured	skipped
woke	giggle	flew	jumped
sat	slithered	plopped	somersaulted
climbed	groaned	ran	stared
washed	gathered	pushed	asked
brushed	said	sing	crawled
is	collected	chattered	moaned
cried	walked	listen	spilled
eating	took	quit	
called	fell	went	

When Hector ______________ up, he rubbed his eyes and ______________ out of bed. "It sure is quiet," Hector said. He ______________ his teeth and dressed in his school clothes. Next he combed his hair. He listened for his sister, Lisette. "It ______________ really quiet," Hector said. "Maybe she's ______________ quiet cereal." Hector collected his homework and books. He ______________ them in his backpack. Hector went into the kitchen. No one was there. "Hello?" Hector ______________ softly. He poured himself a bowl of "Crunchy Critters" and sat down. He forgot the milk. He ______________ to the refrigerator and opened the door. He ______________ the milk on his cereal and bent over to ______________ as his cereal crackled. When he finished his breakfast, he said "Hello?" more loudly this time. "I need a ride to school now," he said. He ______________ into his sister's room. She was snoring softly. "Wake up!" he yelled, "you'll be late for school!" Lisette ______________ up and opened her eyes widely. She stared at Hector. He ______________ back at her. Suddenly she started to laugh, and she ______________ back under her quilt. "Hector," she moaned, "it's *Saturday*!" Hector ______________ too!

Adjectives Revisited

In an earlier section, you learned to make your sentences come alive with describing words called adjectives and adverbs. Now, we will look more closely at adjectives, learning when and where to use them.

Example: Rikki saw a cat.

Can you imagine what kind of cat she saw? If everyone in your class were to take out a piece of paper and draw a picture of the cat that Rikki saw, all the drawings would be different. Here is another sentence about Rikki and the cat:

Rikki saw a large, black cat with sharp fangs.

If everyone in your class drew a picture of this cat, the drawings would be similar. The words that describe the cat that Rikki saw — large, black, and sharp — are called adjectives. As you learned before, adjectives are words that describe people, places, or things.

In the sentences below, your job is to find the adjectives. When you find one, circle it, and then write it in the box below to start your adjective collection. The first one has been done for you.

1. My big, funny brother wears a green uniform when he plays football.
2. I'm going to have blue hair for Halloween.
3. Your house is really nice.
4. Sheila is a tall girl with blue eyes.
5. Did you see that yellow sports car?
6. Your lunch is in that brown bag.
7. This is a yucky sandwich; do you have any good food?
8. I saw a cool movie full of fast cars and wild action.

My Adjective Collection

Find the Adjectives

It's snowing words! Some of the words below are sentence subjects, or nouns (words that name people, places, or things), some are verbs (words that describe action), and some are adjectives (the describing words). Can you find and circle all the adjectives?

beautiful	sneeze	dinner	sticks
baby	playgrounds	swim	funny
cabin	Lisa	red	teacher
jump	skates	pajamas	snow
thick	heavy	wash	slip
car	laugh	Danielle	fuzzy
dog	tree	fast	Mrs. Cole
run	cute	Chicago	stinky
sandwich	shoes	marbles	cry
Mother	dance	hot	cold
book	drive	music	fly
school	little	crazy	slimy
sticky	Jorge	Monday	

Your Turn to Create Adjectives

The story below is missing some adjectives. Can you add them? Write adjectives in the spaces. Think of your own. Some adjectives have already been added for you. They are underlined.

It would soon be Jason's <u>ninth</u> birthday. He was very excited. "This will be the ____________ birthday ever!" he said. What Jason wanted more than anything else was a(n) ____________ bicycle. He had seen one just the <u>other</u> day in the ____________ window of the bike shop. One day, he was looking for a <u>big</u> box in the garage and he found a <u>red</u> scooter hidden under an <u>old</u> blanket.

"Oh!" Jason said. "A scooter! But I want a(n) ____________ bicycle!" He went inside to his room and sat down on his ____________ bed. Jason felt sad. He stayed in his <u>little</u> room and looked at pictures of his family. He could hear them talking in the kitchen.

Jason decided a scooter would make a <u>good</u> birthday gift. The more he thought about it the more excited he got.

Finally the big day arrived. "Happy birthday!" his family said. They took him outside. There was a ____________ box wrapped in ____________ paper. Jason was sure there was a <u>red</u> scooter inside the box. He was excited. When he got the <u>big</u> box open, he peered inside and said, "A bike?"

"Isn't that what you wanted? A(n) ____________ bike?" his dad asked.

Jason felt confused. "I just thought I was getting a <u>red</u> scooter."

"A red scooter?" Jason's ____________ sister cried.

Jason's mom laughed, "You are a <u>silly</u> boy!" she said. His parents winked at each other.

"This is what I *really* wanted, a(n) ____________ bike!"

After Jason's ____________ sister went to sleep, his parents came in and told Jason that the scooter was a surprise for his ____________ sister's ____________ birthday. "I know," Jason said.

"You're a(n) ____________ boy," his dad said.

Matching Adjectives

Cut out the word boxes below and turn them facedown. Invite a classmate or two to play a matching game with you. At each turn, the player turns over two of the pieces. If you turn over a describing word plus a person, place, or thing described, you have a match. Take those pieces for your pile and take another turn. If you have two descriptions or two things, places, or people, turn the pieces back over, and it's the next player's turn. When all the pieces are turned over, the player with the most matches is the winner.

Adjectives

chewy	crazy	gigantic
rough	slippery	fluffy
sweet	skinny	slow
nice	yellow	crummy

People, Places, Things

shoes	caterpillar	fingers
Grandma	Mr. Crabapple	shoelaces
beach	babies	Dad
marshmallows	monsters	dirt

Matching Adjectives *(cont.)*

Adjectives

gooey	sticky	teensy
scary	huge	sharp
shiny	squishy	itchy
crummy	short	plaid

People, Places, Things

baskets	supermarket	Mrs. McGillicutty
chicken	pillow	pumpkin patch
bread	tomato	North Pole
tires	sister	toe

One Sentence at a Time

You can write only one sentence at a time. After writing many, you will have enough sentences to make a story. What if you wrote only the first sentence and had everyone else you know write the rest of the sentences? In this activity, the first sentence has already been written. Your job is to write the second sentence. Find classmates or family members to write the rest of the sentences. Each person should write only one sentence at a time, but if anyone wants to write more, the group should choose an order and take turns. For even more fun, don't let the writers see the sentences that were written before. Read your story aloud to the class when it is completed. Use the back of this page if you need more room.

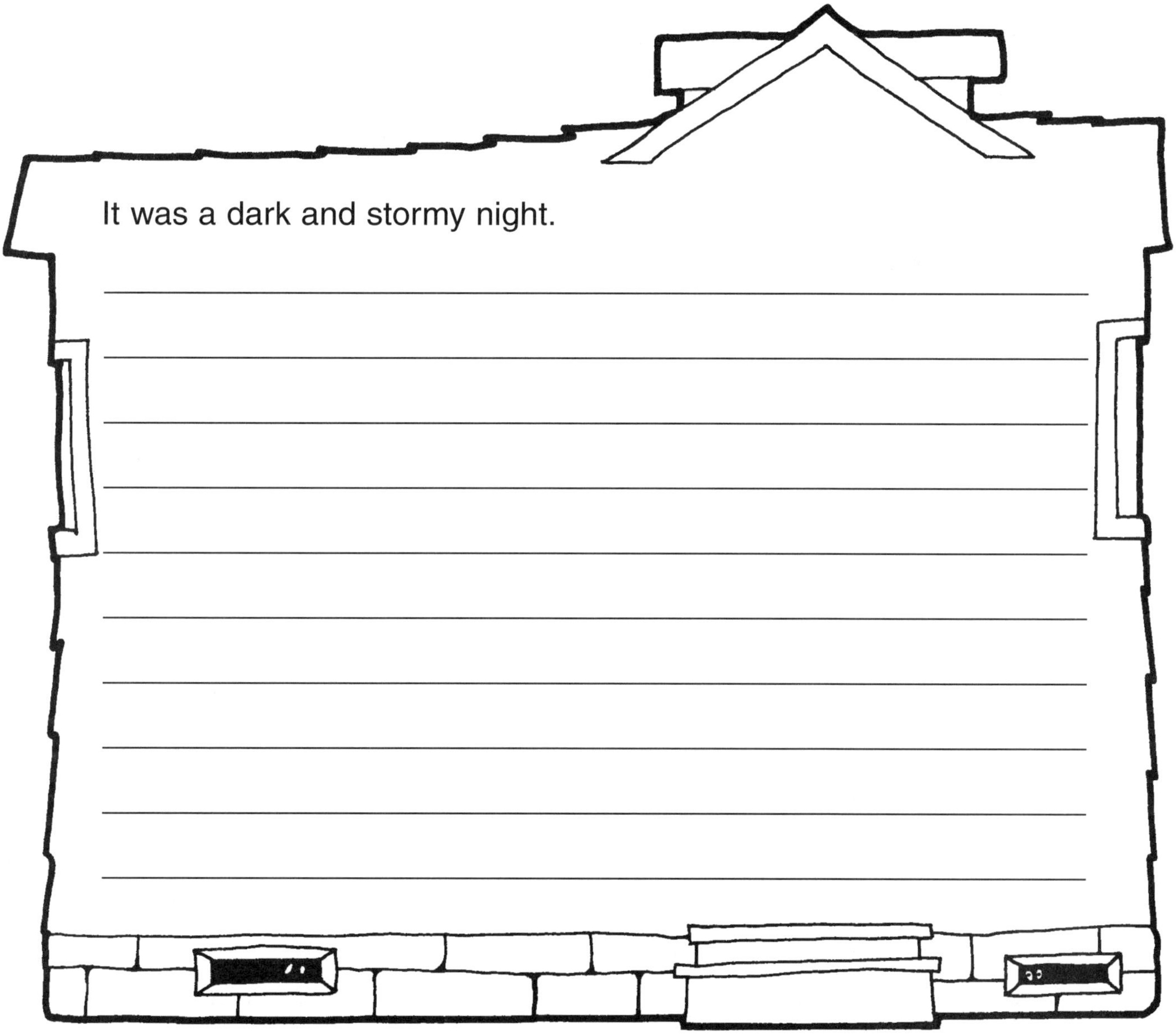

Sentence Maze

What is this girl going to do today? Find out by making a sentence as you go through the maze.

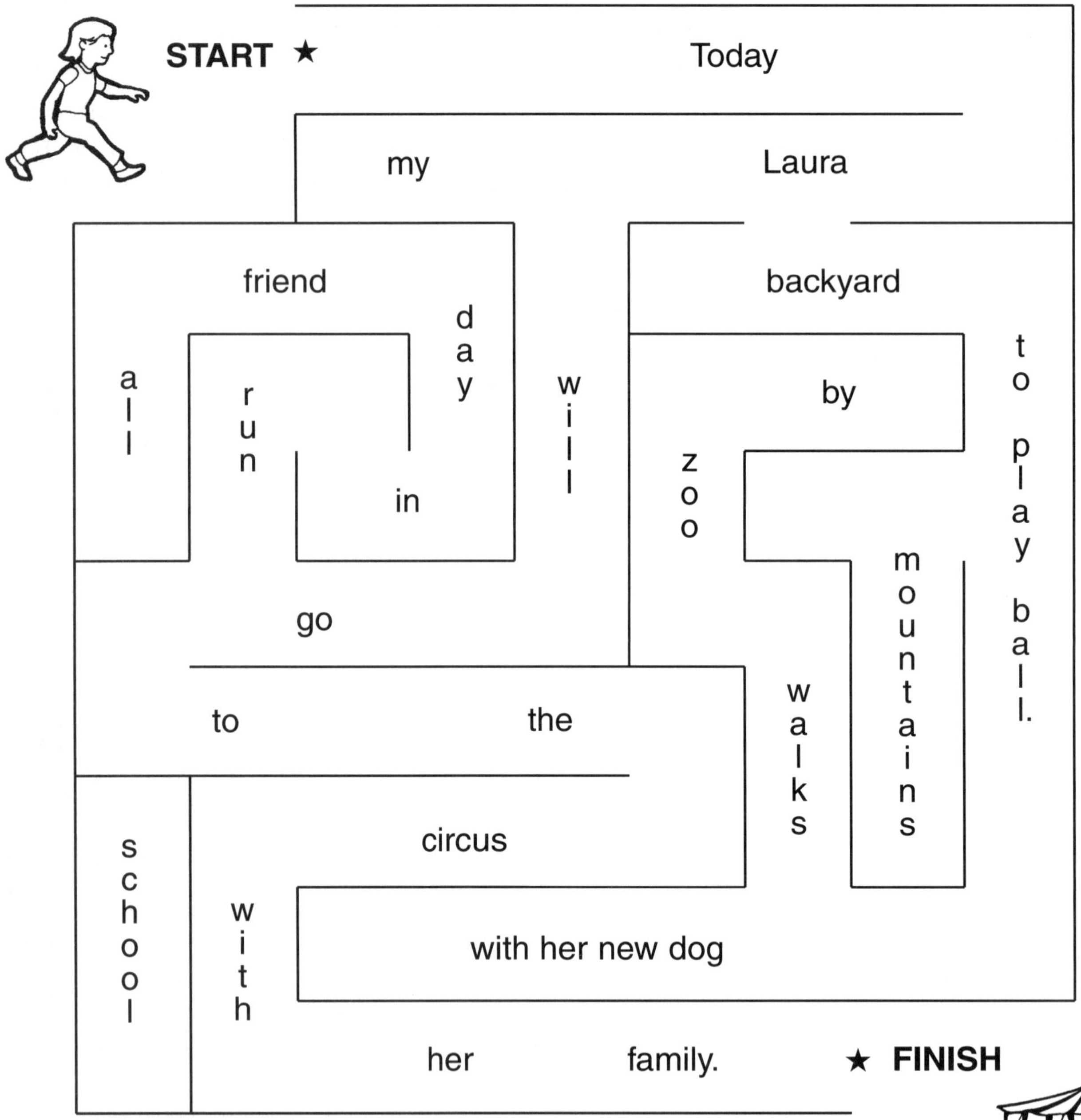

Now write the sentence here.

Silly Sentences

Follow the directions on pages 41–43 to make and play this game. To make the Subject Cards, reproduce this page on red cardstock or sturdy paper, or glue it onto red construction paper. Cut apart the cards. Then make the Verb Cards (page 42) and the Complement Cards (page 43).

My teacher	A big, green monster	My grandmother	A little baby
An alien from Mars	A teddy bear	A dinosaur	A slimy creature
A dog as big as a horse	An orange grasshopper	A cute, little boy	The trash collector
A fuzzy caterpillar	A large, blue car	A rock star	A giant panda

Silly Sentences *(cont.)*

To make the Verb Cards, reproduce this page on blue cardstock or sturdy paper, or glue it onto blue construction paper. Cut apart the cards. Then make the Complement Cards (page 43). Finally, show students how to play the game using the directions on page 43.

jumps	growls	roars	giggles
sits	creeps	swims	sings
rolls	crawls	flies	eats
snores	cries	somersaults	slips

Silly Sentences *(cont.)*

To make the Complement Cards, reproduce this page on orange or yellow cardstock or sturdy paper, or glue it onto orange or yellow construction paper. Cut apart the cards. Then have students follow these directions: Shuffle each set of cards. Place the sets of cards facedown in stacks. Choose one red, one blue, and one orange (or yellow) card. Use the cards to make a sentence. Continue making silly sentences until you find one that you especially like. Write that sentence and use it to create a story.

on my head.	around the world.	in a large bucket of peanut butter.	with my dad.
in the forest.	at the airport.	behind the garage.	under the car.
all the time.	at our house.	in the bathtub.	in the air.
through the school.	on my big toe.	in the classroom.	on a piece of paper.

All About Me!

Now that you can write sentences, it's time to write about yourself. Write five sentences about yourself. Use the idea bank if you can't think of anything to say about yourself.

My name is ______________________________

____

____

____

____

____

____

____

____

____

Idea Bank

- What is your favorite food?
- What do you like to do after school?
- What do you like to do on the weekends?
- What is your favorite sport?
- What do you look like?
- How do you act?
- What is your favorite book?
- How would you change the world?
- What do you wish for?
- Who is your favorite author, and why?
- What are you afraid of?
- What is your favorite subject in school?
- What do you like to wear on your feet?
- Where in the world would you like to go?
- What is your bed like?
- Do you love animals?
- What chores do you do?

Award

Reproduce this award on brightly-colored paper or cardstock. Fill it in and cut it out. You may wish to use scissors that cut with a fancy edge, such as pinking shears.

Congratulate Me!

I Can Write a Sentence!

____

Official Sentence Writer

______________________ ______________________

Teacher Date

Answer Key

Page 7
The following sentences should be circled: 2, 3, 4, 5, 7, 8, 10.

Page 8
The sentences are as follows:
1. Chris is making enchiladas!
2. My dog went ice skating.
3. Stop that runaway bicycle!
4. Kip is washing the dishes.
5. I like Mike!

Page 9
2. Watch out, Kevin!
3. I won a prize!
4. Will you be my best friend?
5. In the morning, I will.
6. What's for lunch?
7. We were taking a bath.
8. A giant dragonfly landed on my head!

Page 10
Answers will vary.

Page 11
3. My teacher is nice. She smiles all day long.
4. I got some new goggles. Do you want to go swimming?
5. My brother is sick. He has to take some nasty-smelling medicine.
6. I have a hamster. Her name is Stella.
7. Pizza is my favorite food. My sister works at Pizzaland.
8. Can I go over to Lan's house? We're going to play space rockets. It's a really fun game. You would like it. Do you want to come and watch us?
9. I got a new bicycle. It is blue and white. It goes really fast. I like it a lot.
10. There is a snake in my classroom at school. I like toads and frogs better. My friend, Nathan, prefers mice.

Page 12
3. I got a new scooter. Wait until you see it!
4. I don't want any soup. It's too hot.
5. My baby brother ate my homework. He was very hungry.
6. Carrie saw a monster in the park. He was afraid of her.
7. My mom got new shoes. I tried them on.
8. My cat scratched me. Do you have a cat?
9. Hector planted some flower seeds. Weeds grew instead of flowers.
10. Can you come to my birthday party? We'll have lots of fun.

Pages 13 and 14
Answers will vary.

Page 15
Sentence revisions may vary but here are some examples:
1. F — Come on, let's go!
2. F — My book is in my backpack.
3. R — I stubbed my big toe. It hurt a lot.
4. F — A yellow airplane is flying by.
5. R — The story was funny. I couldn't check it out of the library. I forgot my library card.

Page 17
Answers will vary.

Page 18
1. Period or exclamation point
2. Exclamation point
3. Question mark
4. Period or exclamation point
5. Question mark
6. Period or exclamation mark
7. Period
8. Question mark
9. Exclamation point
10. Period

Page 20
1. I said, "I don't want to go to the dentist!"
2. I found these things in my backpack: rubber bands, a popsicle stick, a rubber ducky, my dog's leash, a doggie biscuit.

Answer Key *(cont.)*

Page 20 *(cont.)*

3. Do you know how to spell shouldn't?
4. My mom said, "Clean up your room right now, or you won't be going out!"
5. Ouch, that hurt!
6. Tanya, can I talk to you?
7. When my sister saw the spider, she yelled, "Yikes!"
8. The new boy, Jacob, comes from Phoenix, Arizona.
9. I have four pets: a dog, a cat, a goldfish, and an iguana.
10. Help, she's standing on my hair!

Page 21

Answers will vary and are not confined to the word bank.

Page 22

Answers will vary.

Page 23

The following answers should be underlined in the sentences and written in response to the questions.

1. puppies
2. ice cream
3. Jason
4. dad
5. Christy
6. nose
7. baby
8. hair
9. Kip
10. telephone

Page 24

The subjects:

1. mother (or sister)
2. pie
3. sister (or mother)
4. cat
5. television
6. you
7. Blue
8. Summer

Page 25

Answers will vary.

Page 26

3. My dog likes to chew on my shoes
4. Jamie has a tree house.
5. My grandma made me a birthday cake.
6. Tasha swims really fast.
7. I don't like Brussels sprouts.
8. My brother is too noisy.
9. I like to eat fish.
10. Tony's feet are really big!

Page 27

Answers will vary

Page 30

1. has
2. ran
3. has
4. kicks
5. is
6. is
7. jumped
8. screamed
9. is
10. fell

Page 31

The action verbs:

playing
ran
played
counted
yelled
tried
hid
hid
found
looked
looked
was tired
meowed
looked
growled
screamed
laughed
ate
should play
said
ran

Answer Key *(cont.)*

Page 32
The verbs are: run, walk, sleep, jump, fall, tickle, sneeze, kick, hug, and dance.
1–10—Answers will vary.

Page 33
Students may use different verbs to fill in the story, so this is just one way to complete it:
When Hector woke up, he rubbed his eyes and climbed out of bed. "It is sure is quiet," Hector said. He brushed his teeth and dressed in his school clothes. Next, he combed his hair. He listened for his sister, Lisette. "It is really quiet," Hector said. "Maybe she's eating quiet cereal." Hector collected his homework and books. He put them in his backpack. Hector went into the kitchen. No one was there. "Hello?" Hector said softly. He poured himself a bowl of "Crunchy Critters" and sat down. He forgot the milk. He walked to the refrigerator and opened the door. He poured the milk on his cereal and bent over to listen as his cereal crackled. When he finished his breakfast, he said "Hello?" more loudly this time. "I need a ride to school now," he said. He went into his sister's room. She was snoring softly. "Wake up!" he yelled, "you'll be late for school!" Lisette jumped up and opened her eyes widely. She stared at Hector. He stared back at her. Suddenly she started to laugh and she crawled back under her quilt. "Hector," she moaned, "it's Saturday." Hector moaned, too!

Page 34
2. blue
3. nice
4. tall, blue
5. yellow, sports
6. brown
7. yucky, good
8. cool, fast, wild

Page 35
The words that can be used as adjectives are . . .

beautiful
baby
cabin
jump
thick
car
dog
run
sandwich
book
school
sticky
heavy
tree
cute
dance
drive
little
dinner
swim
red
wash
fast
hot
music
crazy
funny
teacher
snow
fuzzy
stinky
cry
cold
fly
slimy

Page 36
Answers will vary.

Page 40
Today Laura will go to the circus with her family.